To my family
past, present, future

TABLE OF CONTENTS

I.

II.

III.

IV.

V.

I.

*Fundamental in the concept of liberty, in the Fourteenth Amendment,
is the dignity of the individual...*

For The Lovings As Appellants

Loving v. Virginia
Oral Arguments
U.S. Supreme Court, 1967

What Holds Us Together

They took the old drawbridge,
plunged it into the bay,
relic into reef, stress cracks

transformed to a sea zoo, sunken girder and truss.
That bridge was strung over the river for a century,
over mid stream bass,

bottom white perch, the Potomac River
fissure between north and south.
The drawbridge melding Maryland to Virginia,

country to commerce,
and like the stray bull shark
that swims up to round snout

safe nursery shallows,
it fords one history to the next.
My grandfather was a traveler

like those who crossed that bridge.
He came over from a farther place,
from Holland, teenaged and pocketless

but he could do figures in his head
faster than fish can hide.
His English was punctuated with Dutch guttural,

the way water grinds rock, mixes cement
that upholds the American dream,
Detroit automobile factories that he designed.

He once slept under a new building
to prove his math,
roofline rafter long like the gray river whale.

...

My husband's grandfather
was a different kind of laboring man.
Dark as slave history, he was strong

like an alloy of carbon and iron,
big man with a chest as wide as the hood of a car.
He worked in the steel mills of Birmingham

where after the Civil War cash from moneymen
flowed like smelting ore,
ore that moved like oil, or red lava,

the kind that creates a new land
from the ocean floor.
From black-red blooms,

those steelmen
turned out the unyielding-I, wide flanges
and giant joists.

And in that old bridge's last sinuous reflection
I am realizing
it is possible

that the I-beam my northern immigrant grandfather
slept under
was made by my husband's grandfather,

steelworker
in an Alabama house of heat.
Once I thought that in marrying, in melding,

welding our families together that I would become
like that drawbridge, or repurposed in an ocean.
But now I know I am more

the slipstream bull gray that has always ventured up river,
nosing for water-weeded eddies
as if to protect our young.

Fireball

Caroline County, Virginia, 1958

it was a very long way   the arrest   as they slept
how it came
out of the dark sleeve of night
like the meteor

that gravity-blasted   caved the crater   hollowed
the bed of bay
clast debris   across the floor
from the fireball

a sheriff may not recall   how the bay was formed
he better knows
when to surprise   lovers at home
not in day   but in the dark uniform of night

                         the tin stars

flashlights   headlights   cruiser lights
Mildred in the cage   of the car
head back
fishhook in the slip of her throat

while always in the bay   the long body of ground water   sinks
into the rim   of salt water
and so he came   at 2 am
the bay   a mixing zone

[The Justice of the Peace] told me...if they are married, arrest them.
I told him I'd be glad to do it.

Woman In Jail With A Week To Think

Day 1
Mildred Loving, Old Pauly Jail
Caroline County, Virginia, 1958

From the native oyster
she knew how to prepare.
The way the bivalve,
inside its shell,
carries a safe of saltwater
to survive
long periods out of the sea.

How Things Are (Not What They Seem)

Alexandria, Virginia, 2003

Even in the way the flat cuttlefish, which is colorblind,
ripples along the English Channel,
its wake like the hem of the petticoat
that Pocahontas wore

or the scalloped riffled
edge of parchment bills,
racial integrity laws
passed on the legislative floor.

So the cuttlefish and its system of cells
can match any background when cued,
blending with algae or sand
under cover of chromatophore.

In a similar way
my children,
when tracked or tallied,
are turned from white to brown
to black or more.

Curious that while staying the same
something can be completely changed,
as with cuttlefish.
When correctly classified as mollusk,
not fish at all, but metaphor.

Into The Headwind

The Lovings of Caroline County, Virginia,
living in exile in Washington, D.C.,
meet with their lawyers, 1963

He was a bricklayer, drag car racer,
his neck ringed with a pattern
like tires, Saturn or the solferino trim

around the rim
of the Lincoln White House china.
E Pluribus Unum, eagle and shield in the center.

At the law office, they sat on the sofa,
Richard's arm behind her
as long as a church pew.

They all said he deferred to her.
Mildred, soft as pressed curls,
her oyster-buttoned sweater,

the neat scroll of her handwritten note —
words like canoes or sailboats
making their way into the headwind.

Exhibit 1: Letter From Mildred Loving
To The American Civil Liberties Union

1151 Neal St. N.E.
Wash. D.C.
June 20, 1963

Dear Sir:

I am writing to you concerning a problem we have.

5 yrs. ago my husband and I were married here in the District. We then returned to Va. to live. My husband is white, I am part negro & part Indian.

At the time, we did not know there was a law in Va. against mixed marriages.

Therefore we were jailed and tried in a little town of Bowling Green.

We were to leave the state to make our home.

The problem is we are not allowed to visit our families. The judge said if we enter the state within the next 30 yrs., that we will have to spend 1 yr. in jail...

Please help us if you can.

A Comet Came To Alexandria

Potomac River
1828-1836

There was a Comet rig
square stern

came then sailed away.
Came up to Alexandria,

then sailed down
through the bay

to New Orleans,
100 black men

stowed closer
than planted seed,

coffles chained,
stacked six feet deep.

*A slave pen as near the Capital
in this, our Great Nation.*

Cash for Negros
both sexes.

Chattel
locked in pairs

like the growing
and slack cycles

of cotton
and corn.

...

The largest slave trade company
in the country

headquartered
here in Alexandria.

Agents,
commissioners,

auctioneers,
brokers,

slave drivers,
soul drivers.

Cornmeal, lard,
peas, meat.

A ration
for the week.

Solomon and Winny Lewis:
shoemaker, sempstress $1500.

Titus:
wheelwright, cooper $700.

Abram:
iron worker, blacksmith $800.

Macon:
drayman, stable hand $800.

The waterfront
is improved by the erection of large

and commodious
wharves.

Topography (Is For Lovers)

For my husband

we are the black Allegheny and Blue Ridge   asleep   side by side

    my old hip rises   out of an equator   where beaked dinosaurs

once grazed   too hot   we shifted   drifted over climates

    and flood zones   then rested   in Atlantic shallows

now west, we stretch   dry   and at the bed's edge

    our legs entwine   stream loads to sea   our feet fossilize

in clam molds   you stroke my head   and as you doze

    your hand   unfolds   far   to our north

drops a tendril   of my hair   quartzone stonecurl   of marine snail

Suite: For Miss Liz

1. Bring Me My Babies

1990

My mother-in-law called for my children
on Saturday
to have with her on Sunday.

My daughters'
black patents
dangled lightly

like their hearts
as they all got
seated in the car.

They rode around,
all around town
and to The Church of Love,

queens in Miss Liz's big car,
dressed, pressed,
hair high, slick as Sunday shoes.

When asked what the difference
was at Miss Liz's church,
the girls would say

that the women sway,
faint
and fall out.

2. Wedding Gift

1985

The way my mother-in-law
Miss Liz, heavy set
with what was right,
would gather herself like inflow clouds

that come on with a storm front.
She would dredge herself up
from her front room chair,
her legs unstable pylons

that would ultimately fail
her swaying pier. In a voice
as smoky as greens,
she would take up the change

that was needed in the world,
laying out nuggets
like catfish pieces on a platter.
As I sat with her

she would declare over
the cumulus of my blonde hair
and all those white people need to
rising against the break wall.

3. Funeral In Full Gospel At The Church of Love

1997

Rolling.

Big brick.

Clapboard ship.

The steeple listed.

To the street corner.

4. Stranded

1997

We held hands

above the hole

in the ground.

Sons and daughters-in-law.

Black pearls and me,

the white bead.

II.

...differences essentially in the shape of the eyes...pigmentation of skin —
such differences are meaningless...They serve no proper legislative purpose.
To state the proposition itself is to expose the utter absurdity of it.

Japanese American Citizens League As *Amicus Curiae*

Loving v. Virginia
U.S. Supreme Court, 1967

What I Mean By Relative Time

Virginia

These are rivers of origin.
In spring, the Atlantic sturgeon,
a rarity, lumbers in from the sea,
across the threshold of the Chesapeake.
Comes in like a longhouse,
up the river to spawn,

nosing the soft substrate
for worms and clams,
its bony body covered with shieldplates
like the cliff walls of the Potomac
channeled in the Pleistocene.

In spring, the herring come.
They navigate up the Rappahannock to nurseries,
the blue-backed
or pewter alewife,
metallic as quartzite points
hafted to fit a spear tip,
the herring as it arrows in.

From the orbit of ocean and deep bay
to spawn in the tidal river flush
comes the rockfish bass,
the grand striper,
heavy as a brig
once packed with dark men,
their hands chained,
joined like rivers
in the history of the watershed.

...

Lured by angler's spoons
and crank baits, the fish drift
amid the sunlit sheaves
in glinting larval shallows.

And in the temporary meanwhile,
the shad arrive.
Come about from wintering
near the northern ice rim
to the Eocene estuarine crater
of the Chesapeake.

They come to feed on copepods and mysids,
come to tail-walk the rolls of the river.
Shad as in American shad,
white shad, hickory shad,
hickory jack,
shad that wait for the slow change,

like the passing of planets,
ice melting into temperate water,
or the English plotting, mooring,
mapping this watercourse.
The shad wait,
then spawn.

The water turns as dark
as the patina of a gun,
or a nation rising out of dank light.
And then the fish are gone,
like the moon, the tide, dominion,
changed but the same, overnight.

Reading And Comprehension Of Virginia History

[She was] the instrument to pursurve
this colonie from death, famine,
and utter confusion.
                    Captain John Smith, 1616

He had been born white, but then
the law made him black.
                    Mott Wood, 1928

Some of these mongrels, finding that they
have been able to sneak in their birth certificates
unchallenged as Indians are now making
a rush to register as white.
                    William A. Plecker, M.D.
                    Registrar, 1912-1946
                    Bureau of Vital Statistics
                    Commonwealth of Virginia

That in 1691 Virginia banished any white man who intermarried
        with a Negro, mulatto or Indian bound or free
That Virginia Indians were categorized as black
That in 1924 there evolved a "Pocahontas defense"
That not more than one-sixteenth Indian qualified as white
That one drop of any other admixture turned a person black
That Asians were black
That color must be registered with the State
That mixed marriages with whites were prohibited, a felony,
        in or moving back from out of State
That Pocahontas was Algonquian, daughter of Powhatan
That Pocahontas married an Englishman
That Pocahontas had a son.

Watershed

Chesapeake Bay tributaries:
Potomac, Rappahannock, James and York:
Virginia's parallel rivers

I thought I knew
    what the river said
        running from mountains to bay —
            but like the oysterman

who tends his seaside garden,
    I am learning how one thing beholds another,
        rivers — a timeline,
            like fish line that leads blooms across

the arc of an arbor:
    canoeing tribesmen on the Thames —
        Confederates joined with Union men —
            spat that feeds the flatworms and mud crabs

so the red horse and spot tail swim.
    Fishermen race their boats in morning,
        cast for low tide bass.
            When their churn calms, canoes come again.

Woman In Jail With A Week To Think

Day 2
Mildred Loving, Old Pauly Jail
Caroline County, Virginia, 1958

in the smallest hour   stars   the mariner's map

then drifting

from Africa

the Gold Coast   Biafra

bioluminescence

tears   of black men and women   forced   to cross the sea

Fugitive

John Wilkes Booth

10th Street, N.W.
Washington, D.C., 1865

As the bullet burrowed from the president's ear to eye, Booth escaped
Ford's Theatre and the Capital on horseback, trailing a broken leg.
He slept, leg set, on the velvet divan of a doctor's house, then hid
for days in a thicket of white pine.

And where the Potomac curved like a playhouse balcony, he sidled
through the ravine to a waiting rowboat to cross over to Virginia, but
the current circled him back. The second try, it welled his boat across
the Potomac. But news had traveled. House after house turned him away.
Booth boarded the last night barge over the Rappahannock into Caroline.
Spring triggered a drove of shad. He feared he had been seen.

The first presidential assassin carried:

> -photographs of his Union fiancée;
> -compass, with golden eagle center;
> -small candle, used;
> -leather diary with tide tables, notes:

> *I do not repent the blow I struck,*
> *I may before my God, but not to man.*
> *I think I have done well.*

Come About

1985

We were two women
> farther apart than one shore to the other

as I sat opposite my mother
> in the tight sailboat.

She held the tiller
> to guide the course and let the line run

to fill the sail with wind.
> It was hard for her to let me do the same.

My fingers trailed portside,
> they traced a wake like the horse mackerel

that tags alongside sun swimmers,
> or the ribbon that tracked the wind

at the top of my mother's trimmed sail.
> She called *come about* and I ducked as the sail's

boom swung to the other side,
> and we changed course.

I had chosen this moment, when we were alone,
> in the lift of the mistling waves,

when the sail traversed overhead,
> had stopped its slack and flap

and filled with new wind,
> when, then, my youth would conclude.

...

I told her how other men bored me,
                     their pedigrees and pinstripes ordinary,

and that we could find in the sun and air of the day
                     a way to disagree

about the black man I wanted to marry. How had I allowed him
                     into my broad reach

if not for her love of discovery, music and art?
                     Or that by keeping true north

and a chart of stars in the watch of her mind,
                     she is never lost?

Or that her eyes hold the light like a blue summer evening
                     that thins over the long shore?

Now, with decades over the waterside and heeling
                     in this summer's dusk and breeze

I hear the chime in her voice, like halyards slacking,
                     slinking on metal masts in the marina.

And as she talks with my husband, my mother's back
                     ever more rounds like the hull of that tender.

Exhibit 2: Letter From Mildred Loving To Her Attorney Mr. Cohen

July 6, 1964
1610 10th Street N.W.
Wash. D.C.

Dear Mr. Cohen:

Hope that you remember us.

We haven't heard anything from you for so long,
we had given up hope.

Now once again we have something to hope for. Since
the "Civil Rights Bill" have [sic] become a Federal Law
is there anything that can really be done for us?

Can they really stop us from visiting Va?...

Bass Fishermen Over The Limit

Alexandria, on the Potomac

The wind around my boat calms the brackish water to ripples
like a slurry of colonial glass,
or with the slight glean of gasoline,
citrine, the color of chapel clerestories. In the quiet,

I remember the silver inkwell that sits
on George Washington's desk, the bowl of it.
With its feathered quill pen, it rests on the desk
like a goose on water, just as the flock reflects in the cove

and my bowrider barely moves under the shadow
of Mount Vernon. The tall house seems a near mirror
of Durham Cathedral, its Norman nave,
quire and transepts, as it triumphs out of the turn

of England's River Wear. There, in the high monastery,
four centuries ago, while barbell and sea trout
swam below, Washington's kinsman kept church records.
Here, bass fishermen slow troll,

come near my spot, then blaze the river, scaring
the geese away. As the birds skim by,
their feet scribe wake-trails
in the way goose feathers were kept flexible in water,

then nibbed to write the Magna Carta,
Declaration, Constitution, Bill of Rights.
The birds land on the far shore, a star-line on the horizon.
Their wavelets turn like soft pages.

...

Fishermen come again to take a corner in my cove.
They'll fish close to finger piers
or under the high echo arch of the bridge. They'll stand
on their casting decks to reel their daily count or creel,

then speed their boats to shore, store their catch
and relaunch for more. The flock alights, streams by,
aligns with cars commuting up the parkway,
over bridges to the Capital.

And up the grand river vista, at the Supreme Court,
in front of the high bench of justice, a tradition
awaits every first case on the appellant attorney's desk —
a souvenir pen with white goose quill.

Fugitive Herself

Mildred Loving

10th Street, N.W.
Washington, D.C., 1964

She waited for spring to escape from the Capital, to return to Caroline.
The shad found their way. Mildred missed the scenery, the velvet light
that trailed through the white pine thicket. She burrowed down, drove
over the Rappahannock, the last leg home. House to house Mildred
hid her family as boarders. She was her own eyes and ears. She feared
her children's horseplay, the doctor. News traveled as fast as a bullet.
A bad fish could trigger jail.

And past the skiffs and barges, where the Potomac curved like the well
of the White House balcony, she circled back to the Capital, to her
current house, set up the street from Ford's Theatre.

Wife, mother of three, kept with her:

-blue-lined notebook paper;
-small white envelopes;
-stamps, new:

Mr. Cohen:

Do you think it would help if I wrote to the President?...

III.

*...that is why I say that the white and colored prohibition...
completely controls the racial picture with which Virginia is faced.*

For The Commonwealth Of Virginia
As Appellee

You have no Indians in Virginia?

The Court

Loving v. Virginia
Oral Arguments
U.S. Supreme Court, 1967

Aubade: For My Mother

1. Color Wheel

Look at the sea. Aqua. Aquamarine.
Blended from yellow with heavy pigment of blue.

Look at the lowland, the horse meadow. Grass green
from primaries of yellow and blue. Blue grass, more blue.

Look at the African Violet. Verdant velveteen
with purple blossom, small gem melded of blue and red.

Take in the light of sky. Blue fused with white. Clean.
Or the sunrise. Primary, Indian red, touched by white.

White, reflecting all wavelengths. Black, of whale skin and baleen,
all colors absorbed. Mixed together, a wash of gray.

Gray, like oysters, opening to mother of pearl, unforeseen,
or radiating fog, clearing with the warming spectrum of sun.

2. New Landscape

The water flooded the page like a Dutch field.
        My mother soaked the high cotton paper,
        then dried it some. She liked how the damp sheet

absorbed the paint, how it let that moment happen.
        Like her countrymen, the Old Masters,
        she readied her brushes,

lined up as though reeds or cattails,
        wooden, as she could be to me,
        yet their sable tips, like her soft hair.

She placed jars of water alongside her work cloths,
        then prepared twists of color,
        creamy cadmium red and yellow, marine blue.

She liked to watch the water
        carry the color as though in a quick trail, a bloodstream.
        She showed me where it worked itself

into the rag, paper taking on pigment.
        Then on her palette she would combine colors,
        one into the other to make a new value,

just as against her early caution,
        I married my husband and mixed her grandchildren.
        But I wanted to trust what she knew. In time

she would stand back to see her painting in new perspective,
        marvel at how the colors blended, then clear
        her brush in a spin of water, to put it to paint again.

There Is A Whale Hanging In The I-95
Caroline County Visitor Center

Eobalaenoptera
Excavated 1991, 14 million years old

She is time suspended.
Found in a bed

       where the ocean ended,
       in the Miocene.

              Baleen jaw lifted,
              dorsal fin boned —

                          a woman's hand.

Woman In Jail With A Week To Think

Day 3
Mildred Loving, Old Pauly Jail
Caroline County, Virginia, 1958

The rise and fall of the river.
The Algonquian,

how they make
their canoes.

They chip away
at chert or quartzite

to make an ax point,
search for

and fell
the best tree.

Then wait for
the river ice

to thaw,
for the water to warm enough

to dig in the cold mud
for icy clams.

Eat them.
Or smoke

to preserve
them,

...

44

saving the palm-sized shell
to scrape out

the tree's
hot pulp,

the smoldering
char.

How long they
control that fire

holding it
at its hottest in the core,

down in the deepest
down in the round

of the wood,
burning out the hollow

burning
until the scorched long log

is transformed
into a boat

and floats,
floats

on the river,
its branches

paired
into oars.

Horsepower

1965

The nose of the manifold
flared with hot air.

The wheels gripped the dirt,
then spun it out, like the talk in town.

Richard owned his stock car with two black men,
and when that Ford

bolted down the summer straightaway,
it left a low stratus cloud,

as if a racehorse breezed the track at dawn.
Test and tune weekdays, Sunday race day:

Try your luck at Sumerduck —
the dragway passed the time.

Speed has no color, only smoke.
The hot rodders, they'd sit in the pit

with their wives between Super Series runs.
Richard's payout that season:

39 trophies, five thousand dollars.
They worked under cover of the big hood,

down in the belly of the engine,
all of their arms dark,

slick with fluid, like stable hands
or veterinarians

there to coax a mare,
mare that revved and trembled,
ready, ready to birth a champion.

As If I Belong

it is beauty the way the land lies as open as the ocean
as it was once the bottom of the ocean and now
the fleets of cars on I-95 fall away
as I exit onto History Land Highway where the sign says

if the white line is on your side do not cross over
here the roadside pines lace the light
the Washington-Burgess route threads through Caroline
Land of Opportunity takes me to the town

of Bowling Green the set back homes lush front lawns
where thoroughbreds grazed
Secretariat
sired by Bold Ruler out of Something Royal

the legend born in Caroline in a stall of red straw
later they gaped at the Triple Crown winner
his dead red heart
it was this engine just huge

but when *TIME Magazine*
named the racehorse *Man of the Year*
they picked the wrong warrior from Caroline
they held Mildred in that box of bars

for five days five nights in the only female cell
told Richard taunted Richard
that an inmate
a strongman from the work yard

would be put in with her
Old Pauly Jail it's now boarded up with a Johnny on the Spot
in the parking lot it might have charm if it wasn't a jail
next to the courthouse in the town square

...

where at the new hot spot Mix House coffee shop
the caramel lattés have steamed away
all but the menu in the window of the Old Courthouse Café
Salt fish and eggs choice of corn bread or grits

but the jewelry store is open a jeweler is an expert
in the proceedings of love the selection of rings and settings
Rhythm of Love TwoGether
the Fingerprint Collection

the jail and courthouse are a very long way from their house
the arrest when they were in bed when the sheriff came at 2 am
cold night cruiser lights
red white red white red white red

later she stood before the high magistrate's chair
Queen Caroline's portrait there
jury chairs
that faced the gallery in the Jeffersonian way

the courthouse in the shadow
of high trees and Caroline's Confederate monument
to commemorate
the valor

and endurance of its soldiers
the cool air tile floor Virginia law
the runaway slave
shall be hired out with an iron collar on his neck

and when Mildred came in from the holding cell
news spread as fast as a spring rivulet runs
turns of every tongue
unlawfully and feloniously

left the state with the purpose of marrying
I pass the sign for Triple Crown Produce
curve and swerve through the narrow rein of roads
to her far country lane

. . .

where the roadside pines line fallow fields
and returning to cohabit as man and wife
where Rappahannocks once hunted
planted beans that twined up the cornstalks

with squash in between so the broad leaves
shaded out the weeds
against the peace and dignity
of the Commonwealth of Virginia

now the trees recede to a far slip of woods
and the pop pop pop
comes on from behind the horizon
and the gray smoke cloud rises from hang fire tank fire

then trails higher as if from a long house a longhouse
Thumbs Up For Our Troops
the infantry that practice war games in her back wood
for Patton Korea Vietnam the War on Terror Iraq Afghanistan

war games on the live firing range
to be at the ready to protect our rights our freedom
Caroline wraps around Fort A.P. Hill ties like an apron
around Garrett's Farm where Booth was gunned down

around Mildred's house a white house the white house
that backs up to the far woods
I miss the open space
and just walking down a country lane

she lived on the narrow gravelly road
the only goal I had was to bring my family back again
the kind the mailman dusts down
to turn on the Tidewater Trail that unfurls

high over the river bank
where horses chestnut and bay gather and canter
in a slow roll below
where steamships churned up after the Civil War

...

where the English encroached and Captain John Smith
and his cartographer
etched Rappahannock villages
and hunting grounds

for his map of 1612 where the meteor the fireball came on
blasted and turned up opened
opened the mouth of the river
Mildred Loving lived on the kind of lane

where a pickup truck with a bumper strip passes
Driver Has No Cash He's Married
and at her four corners on Passing Road
her red church her graveyard hem in the fray of the field

and the old country store slumps over and into itself
fatigued
as everything in all of Caroline is changed
and changeless

the letters on the store façade barely spell
C-E-N-T-R-A-L P-O-I-N-T
and as I drive along her road the neighbors
who are out to rake their yard everyone waves

The Matter Suspended

Fuller v. Commonwealth, 1949,
precedent discovered
to reopen the Loving case

She is a case closed,

      then reopened,

            in a quarry —

                        of chance find.

...an order...adjudicating guilt
but in which the terms...
were not fixed was not a final order...
since the matter was still...
in the breast of the court.

Exhibit 3: Judge Bazile Of Caroline County Responds To The U.S. District Court

Richmond Civil Action No. 4138

affirming his conviction and suspended
sentence of the Lovings and thereby
issuing an appealable ruling, 1965

*Almighty God created the races white, black, yellow, malay
and red, and he placed them on separate continents. And but
for the interference with his arrangement there would be no
cause for such marriages. The fact that he separated the races
shows that he did not intend for the races to mix...*

*Conviction of a felony is a serious matter. You lose your
political rights; and only the government has the power
to restore them...And as long as you live you will be known
as a felony...*

Judgment

Almighty God created

conviction

And as   you live you will be known

IV.

The Lovings have the right to go to sleep at night, knowing that should they not wake in the morning their children will have the right to inherit from them…they have the right to be secure in knowing…

For The Lovings As Appellants

Loving v. Virginia
Oral Arguments
U.S. Supreme Court, 1967

If The White Line Is On Your Side Do Not Cross Over

fully I was told not to share not to share
what I was fully writing about about
when I said it was about deep personal choice about
personal about deep personal choice like which
lane like which direction to go to go to take
which lane to get in which lane

Woman In Jail With A Week To Think

Day 4
Mildred Loving, Old Pauly Jail
Caroline County, Virginia, 1958

The fiddler lays the honeyed body back
for the country dance, cradles its ebony neck,

fingers resonate through the soundboard. So too
the fiddler crab plays, orchestrates, waves

his one large claw to guard his mate. Others
fight to break it off, a discard in the mud flats.

Look at the way under duress the crab draws
water, splits the purfling of its seam to molt,

so a new, ready hand expands,

while the virtuoso tucks the violin close to his waist,
uses the case of his arm to protect his songmaker.

Arioso: For My Father

1. Rest (Unrest)

My father gathered sound
                    in his arms, conducted from the podium.

He looked to the trombones,
                    brass slides slurring in, then out,

the way the longnose pike feeds,
                    then hides in the weeds.

Play without the mute until the sound
                    disintegrates.

With embouchure of lips and lungs that brass row
                    let the sonority drown down

out of the bell, out of the body.
                    Garfish still as a stick.

2. Tempo

Working early and late,
in light like the graphite of his penciling,
my father sat in his studio,
marked the score with clefs,

then began one note and the next.
He propped the sheaths up on the piano
leaning in from the bench,
in thought deep as water,

his robe around him, dark night blue.
On page after page he composed ostinatos,
timbre of trumpet and trombone,
the pages scaled next to each other in crescendi,

others discarded, leaves floating downstream.
When I was young, he let me run my hands
over the clean sheets,
to draw in the measures that ran perpendicular

to the pre-printed five-lined staves.
He gave me the thick metal ruler,
its back stiffened with cork so it would not slip
as it jutted from top to bottom of the page,

my ruled lines new piers or pilings
laid to gird a delicately suspended structure.
At dusk now, as the light turns into night's tone poem,
all that is left of my father is his music. The drawbridge

over my nearby river is lit,
its control tower tall and silvery, the lights across
the bridge span treble notes, a melody,
and in soft rhythm in the deep register of water,
their harmonic reflection.

They Met With Their Royal Street Lawyers

Alexandria's Main Streets:
King, Queen, Prince, Duke and Washington

The law firm sign swings gently, the way Mildred's handbag hinged on her
arm. Now the trolley runs from the river to the Metro, passing the office
on its way. There, the Kiss & Ride drive-through rounds like a soapstone
bowl. Zacarias Moussaoui was tried nearby in Federal Court, the black
Escalades pulled out after midnight under deep pearl light. A few blocks
down, past Whole Foods, the Urban League owns the Franklin & Armfield
site, once the slave trade compound where "fancy" girls, mulatto or
quadroon, were sold to the carnival.

After Hurricane Isabel, CNN canoed up King for their newsfeed; notches
on the Torpedo Factory Arts Center measure the storm surges, this one
was 10 feet. Even as far uptown where Lafayette stayed, carp and catfish
were tossed like baguettes on the cobblestone. During the Civil War,
Lincoln reinforced the wharf against the weather and Confederates with
a large barge of Union soldiers. And the first time his presidential railcar left
the harbor work yard, it was draped in satin mourning.

The afternoon bathes the nave in sun, gilds the commandment plaques in
Christ Church. Washington's and Robert E. Lee's pews open to each other,
the families linked by marriage. Churchill sat in Washington's red velvet seat.
For years, the town honored Lee and Martin Luther King on the same day.
And when emancipated slaves walked up from southern fields to Alexandria,
some used river shells to adorn their small pine boxes. Now the Contrabands
and Freedmen Cemetery aligns with the new I-95 bridge. Recently, from
the outline of a freedman's grave shaft, an archaeologist knelt down
on the hallowed ground and picked up a 13,000-year-old Clovis point, about
the size of an infant's hand.

Lunch: District Taco
Teens shop for summer tops, skirts
First kiss, feather-light

Song

For my husband
1985

Shoremaker

    this beach now knows

your curling caress

    the soft slink of you

Detail From "One Drop" Rule

If there is   one

emerald   anchovy

darting in   the water

the ocean   cannot be blue.

Exhibit 4: Letter From Mildred Loving To Her Attorney Mr. Hirschkop

April 5, 1967
Helmet, VA

Dear Mr. Hirschkop,

We received your letter and are very happy to know about the trial of April 10th.

We would love to come if we could be of any help, but otherwise we wouldn't understand anything and we would just be nervous.

Do you have any idea when a decision will be made?

Without Brains Or Hearts

then comes the time
when wind and tide
bring sea nettles, threats
into the bay,
their soft bodies,
tentacles

           as deceptive
           as the silent 'c'
           that begins
           the comb jelly's name
           ctenophore —
           that requires
           my children's caution

I share that jellyfish,
other menaces,
live without brains
or hearts,
and will entangle
burn or paralyze

           but I also show
           how some in the sea
           have become immune,
           the spider crab
           that sits on the medusa head

           the harvest fish,
           butterfish —
           they swim
           amid stingers
           as if through young girls' hair

Magnetism

For my oldest daughter

in drift morning
night drag
my dense core
rolled drum sound

mantle muscled
my skin taut
continents
conjoined in

white belly earth round
until you child
landlet
born from the spread

of my seafloor
your father
carbon constant
my true sun

my opposite
a new land mass
your slab smooth
skin stretched

as bone-plates move
is your life
to be a rough rift
my fault line

from tectonic shift
or will you tip
our slow world
to a hip axis?

Often When My Daughter Sleeps

For my youngest daughter

Her arms lie above her head,
as if reaching for light,

as though she is eelgrass
floating

in a great underwater meadow
where the lined seahorse,

blue crab and bass hide.
Perhaps she is part

of a submerged river forest, reaching,
like pine in pre-Columbian time,

that once covered the watershed.
She is tender biota

in that bed.
Often, when she wakes

her face
is salted with moisture.

In The Breast Of The Court

From the ruling that eventually
allowed *Loving v. Virginia* to be
appealed and rise to the Supreme Court, 1967

He was enchanted by his Queen,
her lovelocks entwined with pearls,
face as ivory as the cameos she wore.
In summer, at Hampton Court, her whale-boned hoopskirt
and private apartments opened to his voice:
eight children, one stillborn.
In his privy garden by the loop of the River Thames,
King George II contemplated his choice of horses,
trumpet songs, maidens to bed,
his German heritage and the mixed marriage
of his House of Hanover on the British throne.
He took his lead from his engaging Queen —
her love of discourse, courtly dance, music, art, the stars —
her hand's firm command on the kingdom
when they were apart.
He bestowed her name, Caroline, for a new county
in his Virginia colony, then, on his deathbed,
ordered the sides of their coffins removed —
last monarchs buried in Westminster Abbey —
so in dust their dust could mingle

But does His Majesty approve of his Queen's portrait
hung in the Caroline courthouse —
brushwork from the finest horsehair —
there above the Virginia judge's chair?
In oil impasto, Caroline's regal hand opens to grace
the crown on table display —
in the way the King once traced
the arch of her back to the rise of her neck —
their pulse to the cup of her breast —
in the painting her hand lightly rests, protects the crown,
its cross and aquamarine monde.

...

And in an event that echoes like the footsteps
of new arrivals who cross the Abbey floor,
kingpins of the Commonwealth
ordered a young couple —
Richard, wife Mildred,
her curls pressed as soft as a royal robe —
brought them in on a trumpeted charge of mixed marriage
for a handcuffed cameo before a judge
in the Rappahannock watershed —
where bivalves — river jewels — cup the past, scour it new —
brought them in to stand before the Queen's remembrance
in the court that bears Caroline's name.

Now as I live in the history of how our bed is made
my husband courts me in night's rich brocade
by our Potomac River's bend.
His arms enrobe me in dark velvet as mine rope over him —
the luster of Caroline's pearls —
just as rivers — and their stories — join and flow to the bay.
We breathe and sleep as deep as the whales
in their ocean opera house,
in the work of our own, in the memory of other marriages,
and the Supreme Court case with more dead ends
and loops than the palace garden maze —
when Richard Loving ordered his Royal Street lawyers
to state his loyalty in life:
tell the court I love my wife.

V.

...if the State is urging here that there is some State principle of theirs: what is it? What is the state of the danger to the people of interracial marriage?

For The Lovings As Appellants

Loving v. Virginia
Oral Arguments
U.S. Supreme Court, 1967

Letter To My Daughters

The Lovings were arrested the year I was born.

My mother taught me reverence for nature.

Sheriff Brooks told *The New York Times*, "If they'd been outstanding
people, I would have thought something about it, but with the caliber
of those people it didn't matter. They were both low class."

30 of the 48 states passed antimiscegenation laws.

I first learned of the Loving case reading Mildred's 2008 obituary.

When I brought you to visit San Miguel, you were presumed
to be Mexican.

Both lawyers served pro bono.

My violin has white tuning pegs.

Someone poured sugar down the gas tank.

When Washington died at Mount Vernon, he had 317 slaves.

Grandma Liz styled your hair with Vaseline for church.

The D.C. boardinghouse where Booth loaded his Deringer with the small
lead ball is now Wok and Roll Restaurant and Karaoke.

If the mountains of Virginia had used their greatest torque, the east coast
of America would be Africa's western shore.

There is no horse race in humanity.

Grandma Liz dragged and pushed those mattresses up against her front
window. Your father, just five.

The bricks, glass, the water cannons.

What Pew Research On Interracial Marriage Doesn't Say In Its Findings (That One In Six New U.S. Marriages Is Interracial Or Interethnic)

2017

Our daughters

are happy

when summer comes.

Legs already tanned for shorts and skirts.

Woman In Jail With A Week To Think

Day 5
Mildred Loving, Old Pauly Jail
Caroline County, Virginia, 1958

Dig the sand.
Mold with limonite
and crushed midden
(discarded shell mounds,
moons in the ground).

Before the pot dries
wrap it
with knotted net
or plaited cloth,
pressing pattern on the body.

Or with reed,
inscribe it.
Punctuate
the round of the lip.
So the vessel may speak.

The Case Of A Modest Homemaker
And Her Bricklayer-Drag Racer Husband

Loving v. Virginia, 1967

Abomination
amalgamation
assassination
banishment
bead work
black codes
Bombingham
Cambodia
cohabitation
Cold War
Cuban missile
demography
Dred Scott
Du Bois
due process
emancipation
enforcement
eugenics
fire fishing
Freedom Riders
full faith
Green Beret
Great Society
Ho Chi Minh
hot day
Indochina
inheritance
internment
JFK
KKK
LBJ
MLK
manumission
March on Washington
Naim v. Naim   ...

napalm
Nisei
North Vietnam
onion skin
opinion
petition
prison
property
pseudoscience
purity
quartermaster
rain maker
Red scare
redskins
Redskins
restraining order
Saigon
Sansei
servitude
sterilize
South Africa
tobacco
torture
trade beads
tribal council
treaties
UNESCO Statement on the Nature of Race
United Indians of Virginia
Universal Declaration of Human Rights
Vietnam
Viet Cong
Virginia codes
Virginia Company
Warren Court
xenophobes
Your Honors

the humblest is the peer of the most powerful

Exhibit 5: From The Ruling By The U.S. Supreme Court

Loving v. Virginia

Mr. Chief Justice Warren
delivered the unanimous opinion
of the court, 1967

*In upholding the constitutionality of these provisions...
the state court concluded...(their) purposes were to preserve
racial integrity...prevent "the corruption of blood," "a mongrel
breed of citizens," and "the obliteration of racial pride," obviously
an endorsement of the doctrine of White Supremacy.*

*Marriage is one of the "basic rights of man," fundamental to our
very existence and survival. To deny this fundamental freedom
on so unsupportable a basis as the racial classifications embodied
in these statutes, classifications so directly subversive of the
principle of equality at the heart of the Fourteenth Amendment,
is surely to deprive all the State's citizens of liberty without due
process of law.*

*The Fourteenth Amendment requires that the freedom of choice
to marry not be restricted by invidious racial discriminations.
Under our Constitution, the freedom to marry, or not marry,
a person of another race resides with the individual, and
cannot be infringed by the State.*

These convictions must be reversed. It is so ordered.

Velocity

1975

The black crows / the brown cows / Richard drove /

every day / past the soybean fields / the barley / wheat /

the corn / past English Acres / Promise Land Farm /

Triple Crown Produce / he drove this way / nearly every day /

watched for hunters / in bow season / their dead black bears /

like feed sacks in back / ditched trucks / in deer season /

in case the buck / or July dogs shot out / he drove down /

the gravelway / then back / the same way / every day /

for the bricks he laid / house he built / woman he loved /

or he took / the big right turn / that rolled / onto the Tidewater Trail /

that looped / past the horses / loping / in the lowland /

past the grand homes / on the riverbank /

with windows that gleamed / like big wet stones / another day /

he drove / a driver / and then a drunk driver / zagged head on /

Meditation On Matters Of Time

When the mountain stood alone dressed in her dark trees,
the river slowed its momentum to the bay,
algae matted the sun that fed the sea —
the jimmy no longer carried his she-crab.

When the river slowed its momentum to the bay,
the cownose ray lost the current of its prey,
the jimmy no longer carried his she-crab,
the bristleworm shed no eggs.

As the rays nosed, scoured for prey —
soft and hard shell clams scarce —
the bristleworm bore no eggs,
and the blacktip swam in fishless water.

But when clams hard-dig their shells in sand,
sea grasses begin to comb their soft beds,
then blacktip and bull join the basking shark overhead
and whelks whorl their spiraled shells.

When sea grasses comb their soft beds,
the river regains momentum to the bay
then the whole sea whirls, whelk-like, world-like —
and the mountain unfurls her dress of green trees.

Excerpts From The English Dictionary

Pass, passage, passing (v+ing).
Pass sb1 extant L. passus.

Passing Road
Central Point, Virginia

Promise, given between two persons.

To cross a river by ford, ferry, bridge.

To pass for, as something else.

To experience a way of treatment, to suffer "through impassable ground."

Law, act or resolution that commands a nation.

To successfully go through a trial, be approved by a court, legislative sanction.

Come about. Bring to an end. Satisfy the requisite standard.

To proceed past, "complete a voyage."

Canto, song. Section of book or poem.

Passage, aisle in a church.

Depart from life, esp. "to pass to God, or heaven."

Give or tender, the act of passing, convey from one to another.

To inherit, pass or passage.

To serve as mouth of the river.

Lay Me In Your Ground

Passing Road
Central Point, Virginia, 2008

The church
at the end of her lane.

Buried
where she could not marry.

Women Of The Chesapeake

For Mildred Loving

Each heart
an estuary
aorta and vein
riverine channels
cells and platelets
circulate
as though drum
and stripers
saltwater churns with fresh
in beat with the inlet sea

Now the chambers
of my heart
fill more slowly
rise
with systolic tide
your body
lies low
in the aquifer
memory of you
runs in the watershed

In Seeking Understanding

In evening

the beach walk

air

sky

the sleeve

of sunset

as it jackets

the seascape

Then darkness

then darkness

reveals

how seeing

outward

becomes the same

as looking

within

Portrait

The beach slides to tide, curves along its edge,
        a coastline. Surf fishermen cast back,

then far into sloughs and deep water bowls.
        They see sand shift. Shore that was here

is now partly filled by seawater,
        and like a flat, gray skate inadvertently caught,

a pool hovers with a tail that flows back into swash,
        ridge and runnel foreshadowing

an inlet, submerged car park —
        shuttles to the beach for all but earliest anglers.

Backwash, sea rise, tidal range,
        groundwater — all grind sandbanks. Collapsed cliffs

are more evidence for rod men, geologists' conclusions —
        Our Chesapeake *has one of the highest tidewater erosions* —

I have even seen marsh margin, resistant rhizomes —
        last barrier girded by strong peat —

I have seen it overwashed by a perched water table,
        the fetch of waves.

The Atlantic *has been changing the nation's profile*
        for thousands of years. Transforming shore,

the beachface — an impermanent veneer —
        like malleable truths used to salt human differences.

Surf casters know
        the catch today will not be the same tomorrow.

VIRGINIA AND THE CHESAPEAKE BAY REGION

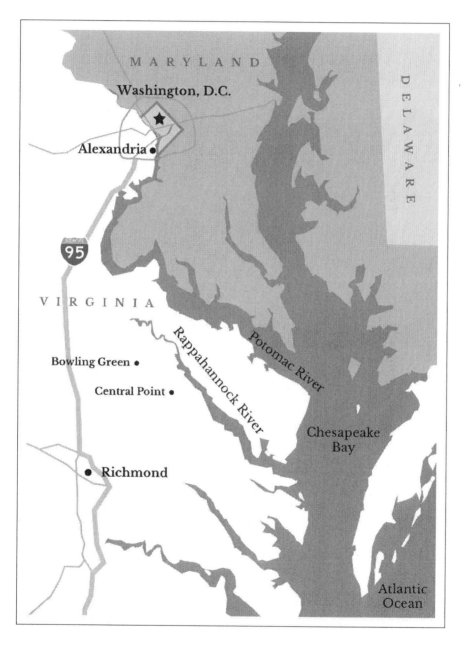

NOTES

"Fireball"
There are numerous geologic clues that a giant meteor caved the crater that
formed the Chesapeake Bay: the brine mix that flows in coastal plain
aquifers and wells, fossils found in jumbled beds on the coast out of geologic
time order, and a large rubble field of molten glass beads — tektites — strewn
to Cuba, and possibly to the tip of South America. The related blast force also
changed the course of the Rappahannock River, so that its mouth turned
upward, against the Bay current. The ending quote of the poem is attributed
to Sheriff Garnett Brooks (Associated Press, June 10, 2007).

"Reading And Comprehension Of Virginia History"
Mildred Loving's birth certificate classified her as Negro, yet in numerous
documents she also identifies as Indian. The Lovings' daughter, Peggy,
confirmed to me that her mother identified as African American and
Rappahannock. In 1608, Captain John Smith mapped 14 Rappahannock
communities along the river. The Rappahannock language was passed
from the Algonquian, of which Powhatan, father of Pocahontas, was
paramount chief.

"Watershed"
Numerous sources record sightings of American Indians on the Thames.
And while accounts of Pocahontas' life often contradict each other in written
and oral British, Virginia, and tribal history, documentation exists of her
introductions at the court of King James, and her life and burial in England.

"Woman In Jail With A Week To Think, Day 2"
From 1657-1708 over 300 slaves arrived to the Potomac Valley. As tobacco
production rapidly increased so did labor demand with wealthy owners
joining to pay for slaving voyages from West Africa. Plantations spread
throughout the Rappahannock and Potomac regions, owned by the
Washington and Lee families, and others. As exhaustion of the land became
apparent, Washington expanded his enterprise to a whiskey distillery,
granaries and fisheries.

"Horsepower,"
"As If I Belong"
Caroline County is known as the birthplace of thoroughbred racing
in America, a claim that spanned from the 1600s when horses were
imported from England to the birth of Secretariat in 1970 at Meadow
Farm. Secretariat's large heart remains a fascination attributed to lineage
that includes an English broodmare from the 1800s named Pocahontas.
But the county's history with horses goes back much further, with tapir and
Callippus fossils from the Miocene found in the Caroline County quarry.

"Woman In Jail With A Week To Think, Day 4"
The Lovings enjoyed house parties where Mildred Loving's brother played
the fiddle. Country dances are a distillation of courtly dances brought
by the British. Queen Caroline, for which Caroline County is named,
was a patron of the composer George Frideric Handel, and she entertained
with music and court dances. In the Lovings' day, people of differing races
could socialize in Caroline County at car rallies, horse races and fiddler
dances. Richard Loving suggested to *Life*, "It never was like a lot of other
places. It doesn't matter to folks around here."

"They Met With Their Royal Street Lawyers"
The poem honors William Marutani, an Asian-American lawyer who
presented oral arguments during the Loving trial before the Supreme Court
on behalf of the Japanese American Citizens League. Formerly
incarcerated at an internment camp for Japanese in northern California,
Marutani argued before Chief Justice Earl Warren and the Supreme Court
on the unequal application of related laws based on race, ethnicity and
religion. As Attorney General of California, Earl Warren had advocated for
the removal of more than 100,000 people of Japanese heritage from their
homes to internment camps. Years later, Warren issued a statement
of regret.

"In The Breast Of The Court"
The burial site of George II and Queen Caroline of Ansbach is marked
by gold inscription in the center of the black and white marble-patterned
floor of Westminster Abbey's Henry VII Chapel.

"Letter To My Daughters"
Like many black Americans in the Great Migration, Miss Liz left
Birmingham, Alabama and the segregated South as a young woman, taking
a bus north in pursuit of opportunity. What she found when she first lived
in Rochester, New York was racial tension that erupted into riots
so explosive that Governor Rockefeller brought in the National Guard,
the first time troops were called into a northern city since the Civil War.

"The Case Of A Modest Homemaker
And Her Bricklayer-Drag Racer Husband"
In 1896 in *Plessy v. Ferguson*, the Supreme Court upheld the
"separate but equal" concept and recognized laws against interracial
marriage "as within the police power of the state." The last line of the
poem is taken from the dissenting opinion by Justice John Marshall
Harlan II: "Our Constitution is color blind."

CASE OVERVIEW: *Loving v. Virginia*

On the occasion of its 50th anniversary, the ramifications of the *Loving v. Virginia* ruling have been widely recognized as going far beyond protecting freedom of choice in relationships and serving as precedent to the 2015 marriage equality ruling. A tribute in *The Atlantic* suggests *Loving v. Virginia* "implores us to reject the eugenic and supremacist remnants of a distant past and to pursue a more diverse, equitable and inclusive society."

The Loving decision repudiated 300 years of slavery-based marriage law. Alabama was the last state to remove antimiscegenation laws from its books in 2000. *Loving v. Virginia* presented a constitutional question to the U.S. Supreme Court: whether laws of the State of Virginia to prevent marriages between persons solely on the basis of racial classifications violated the Equal Protection and Due Process Clauses of the Fourteenth Amendment. On the 40th anniversary of the ruling, Mildred Loving issued a statement, "I believe all Americans, no matter their race, no matter their sex, no matter their sexual orientation, should have the same freedom to marry."

Mildred and Richard Loving grew up seven miles apart in Central Point, a hamlet in Caroline County, Virginia, attending different schools and churches. Their families lived for generations in Caroline, where many community members are of mixed race. When Mildred and Richard's friendship developed into romance their being together was accepted in their circle. Their marriage and subsequent legal proceedings became local and national news.

Richard picked out their officiant from the D.C. phone book. At the time, Virginia's antimiscegenation laws made it illegal for people of differing races to marry in or outside the state and then return. Mildred Loving later offered that she was unaware such marriage was illegal and thought marrying in the District would result in less "red tape."

In the early hours of July 11, 1958, Caroline County Sheriff Garnett Brooks led the raid to arrest the Lovings while they were sleeping. The Lovings were charged and taken to the town of Bowling Green. Richard was released from custody after a night, but Mildred was jailed for five days. While out on bond they could not live together as a family in Virginia. Later that year, Judge Leon Bazile sentenced them to one year in jail, suspending the sentence for 25 years on the condition that the Lovings not return to Virginia together, effectively banishing them.

The Loving case seemed procedurally dead. An early, key question was how to get a case where a guilty plea had been entered back before the court. In working the case, their first year out of law school, Loving attorneys Bernard Cohen and Philip Hirschkop found precedent in *Fuller v. Commonwealth* in which a sentence adjudicating guilt but in which the terms were not fixed was still considered to be "in the breast of the court."

In trying to reopen the case, Cohen filed a motion in Caroline County Circuit Court in 1963 to vacate or annul both the conviction and sentencing. Hirschkop recalled to *Richmond Magazine* (2016) that the case "was more than an average criminal case," and that he was concerned about the risk of resentencing. He added, "You wouldn't be successful challenging just the sentencing, but you had to attack the constitutionality of the statute under which they were sentenced."

Judge Bazile dragged his feet in responding. Cohen and Hirschkop brought a class action suit to the U.S. District Court, Eastern District of Virginia, requesting that a three-judge panel convene to review the constitutionality of Virginia's statutory schemes. The three-judge panel gave the state court 90 days to return an opinion or the case would move to federal court. Judge Bazile understood the consequence of the federal panel deadline and issued a scathing ruling with the preamble of, "they are guilty of a most serious crime."

With the conviction and sentencing affirmed, only then was the case able to move on. Cohen suggested, "what Judge Bazile did when he issued that racist opinion was give us a clear shot to appeal to the Supreme Court of Virginia. We appealed to the Supreme Court of Virginia, got another terrible decision denying us relief, and then had an appealable order from there to the U.S. Supreme Court" (VirginiaHumanities.org). Although the U.S. Supreme Court accepted only one in 400 cases, given its then-recent *Brown v. Board* ruling, Cohen remained optimistic the case would be heard.

On June 12, 1967, nine years after the Lovings were arrested, the Supreme Court ruling reversed their convictions and affirmed the unenumerated right of marriage as "one of the basic civil rights of man."

ACKNOWLEDGMENTS

I offer deepest thanks to the many sources who assisted me with
background research for this collection:

KEY PRIMARY SOURCES and EXPERTS

Bernard Cohen, attorney for the Lovings, who provided extensive background,
follow-up material and personal perspective;

Philip Hirschkop, attorney for the Lovings, for offering a wide lens on
the cultural context of the case, and clarity on legal points and detail that
shaped many poems;

*Michael Johnson, senior archaeologist, Fairfax County, Virginia, and Virginia's study
on Clovis spear points,* for expertise on Virginia's geological past and its impact
on the ecosystem of the Chesapeake;

Peggy Loving Fortune, daughter of Richard and Mildred Loving, who, at the
American Film Institute in an audience Q&A and after, provided answers
to questions that I could not fully resolve elsewhere, including confirming
that her mother identified as African American and Rappahannock.

ARCHIVAL MATERIAL and ARCHIVISTS

Supreme Court trial transcript material
U.S. Supreme Court Archives, Law Library of Congress librarians
for their work with me on our hands and knees to locate critical case
microfiche files;

Case documents, letters, onion skins, notes, marginalia
Central Rappahannock Heritage Center volunteer archivists
who assisted me with the review of court records for the case;

Letters written by Mildred Loving, provided by Philip Hirschkop
and used with guidance and permission from Bernard Cohen and
Philip Hirschkop, attorneys for the Lovings.

BOOKS AND ARTICLES

In order that readers may share in my path of discovery, I offer a reference list that roughly follows my imperfect notes on the sources and materials I found most essential:

On American history important to specific sections:

Bill Glauber, *It was like he was flying: in five weeks in 1973, Secretariat went from a potentially great horse to a racing legend.* Los Angeles Times (1993); James O. Hall, *John Wilkes Booth's Escape Route.* The Surratt Society (2000); John Edwin Mason, Grey Villet, interracial love, and drag racing, 1965. *John Edwin Mason: Documentary, Motorsports, Photo history,* http://johnedwinmason.typepad.com (2012); Sally A. Schehl and Carlo J. Rosati, eds., *The Booth Deringer — genuine artifact or replica?* Federal Bureau of Investigation (2001); Marshall Wingfield, *A History of Caroline County, Virginia: From its formation in 1727 to 1924* (1924).

On *Loving v. Virginia* and its legacy:

_____The crime of being married. *Life Magazine* (1966); Phyl Newbeck, *Virginia Hasn't Always Been For Lovers: Interracial Marriage Bans and the Case of Richard and Mildred Loving* (2004); Gretchen Livingston and Anna Brown, *Intermarriage in the U.S. 50 Years After Loving v. Virginia.* Pew Research Center (2017); Osagie K. Obasogie, *Was Loving v. Virginia really about love?"* The Atlantic Monthly Group (2017); Peter Wallenstein, *Tell the Court I Love My Wife: Race, Marriage and Law — An American History* (2002), and *Race, marriage and the Supreme Court from Pace v. Alabama (1883)* to *Loving v. Virginia (1967) Journal of Supreme Court History* (1998).

On race, black laws, racial purity and the history of whiteness:

June Purcell Guild, ed., *Black Laws of Virginia: A Summary of the Legislative Acts of Virginia Concerning Negroes from Earliest Times to the Present* (1936, 1969); Manning Marable, et al., eds., *Racializing Justice, Disenfranchising Lives: The Racism, Criminal Justice and Law Reader* (2007); Paula Rothenberg, ed., *White Privilege: Essential Readings on the Other Side of Racism* (2004).

On Virginia Indians:

Stephen R. Potter, *Commoners, Tribute, and Chiefs: The Development of Algonquian Culture in the Potomac Valley* (1993); Helen C. Rountree, *Pocahontas's People: The Powhatan Indians of Virginia through Four Centuries* (1990) and *The Powhatan Indians of Virginia: Their Traditional Culture* (1992).

On the watersheds of Virginia, the Chesapeake Bay and mid-Atlantic:

____*Sediment in the Chesapeake Bay and management issues: tidal erosion processes.* Chesapeake Bay Program (2005); John V. Merriner, *Anadromous fishes of the Potomac Estuary.* Virginia Institute of Marine Science; D.S. Powars and T.S. Bruce, *The effects of the Chesapeake Bay impact crater on the geological framework and correlation of hydrogeologic units of the lower York-James Peninsula, Virginia.* U.S. Geological Survey (1999); Peter S. Rosen, *Erosion susceptibility of the Virginia Chesapeake Bay shoreline.* Virginia Institute of Marine Science; Martin Tillet, *Origin of Mount Vernon watersheds.* Mount Vernon Gazette (2014).

FILM, PHOTOGRAPHY, SPECIAL EXHIBITIONS

____*Discovering Alexandria, The Early Years* and *The 20ᵗʰ Century.* WETA-TV, Arlington, Virginia (2016).

___*With Malice Toward None: The Abraham Lincoln Bicentennial Exhibition* Library of Congress, Washington, D.C. (2009).

Nancy Buirski, *The Loving Story.* Augusta Films and HBO, American Film Institute, SilverDocs (2011).

Gray Villet, *The Loving Story Photography.* International Center of Photography, New York, New York (2012).

COLLECTIONS AND EXHIBITS

I also visited, consulted with, or used materials and websites from various entities. Thank you to the scholars, staff and community members who spoke with me to inform the making of this book.

Alexandria Black History Museum
The American Civil War Museum
The British Library/Treasures of the British Library
Captain John Smith Chesapeake National Historic Trail
Caroline County District Court
Caroline County Historical Society
Chesapeake Bay Foundation
Contrabands and Freedmen Cemetery, Alexandria, Virginia
Durham Cathedral
Ford's Theatre Museum and Petersen House
George Washington's Mount Vernon Estate
Historic Royal Palaces: Hampton Court and Kensington Palace
Library of Virginia
Martin Marietta Carmel Church Quarry
Meadow Event Park, Virginia Farm Bureau Federation
Northern Virginia Urban League/Freedom House Museum
Office of the Secretary of the Commonwealth, Virginia Indians
The Rappahannock Tribal Website: Tribal Center
University of Oxford, Ashmolean Museum of Art and Archaeology
U.S. Department of the Army Fort A.P. Hill
U.S. Department of the Interior, Fish and Wildlife Service
Smithsonian Institution, National Museum of African American
        History and Culture
Smithsonian Institution, National Museum of the American Indian
The Surratt Society's John Wilkes Booth's Escape Route Tour
Town of Bowling Green, Virginia
Valentine Richmond History Center
Virginia Council on Indians
Virginia Department of Conservation and Recreation
Virginia Department of Game and Inland Fisheries
Virginia Department of Historic Resources
Virginia Institute of Marine Science
Westminster Abbey
Wok and Roll Restaurant and Karaoke, Washington, D.C.

FELLOWSHIPS, RESIDENCY AND PUBLICATIONS

I am grateful to *The Gettysburg Review*, Mid Atlantic Arts Foundation and the Virginia Center for the Creative Arts for the fellowships and residency they extended in support of the poems in this collection.

Thank you to the editors of the following publications where these poems appeared in the same or similar form:

Beltway Poetry Quarterly, Featured Poet, Nominated for Best of the Net:
"Into The Headwind"
"Reading And Comprehension Of Virginia History"
"One Drop Rule"
"Often When My Daughter Sleeps"
"Portrait"

Beltway Poetry Quarterly, Langston Hughes Tribute Issue:
"Color Wheel"

The Chattahoochee Review:
"New Landscape"

Innisfree Poetry Journal:
"What I Mean By Relative Time"
"Watershed"

IthacaLit:
"Woman In Jail With A Week To Think, Day 1"

Little Patuxent Review:
"How Things Are (Not What They Seem)"

Northern Virginia Review:
"What Holds Us Together"
"Woman In Jail With A Week To Think, Day 5"

Subtropics:
"Tempo"

APPRECIATIONS

My gratitude also goes to writing faculty who taught me purpose in poems, especially A. R. Ammons, Earle Birney, Michael Collier, Cornelius Eady, Terrance Hayes, Stanley Plumly, Sidney Wade and C. K. Williams.

I also wish to thank Charles Jensen for his first reads and inspirational understanding of the long sequence; Grace Cavalieri and Kim Roberts for their valuable guidance and support; my writing circle, especially Margaret Mackinnon and Ann Rayburn, for their advice and steadfast encouragement; Margaret Corum for her editorial intuition; Marcy Gray for her talent and indefatigable commitment as my lead editor; Kumi Korf, Carol O'Brien and Paul Willsea for their generosity; and my daughters for their expertise, observations and many offerings.

Finally, I thank my husband for the many ways he helped bring this book into being; my parents, extended family and friends for their support, love and listening; and Andy for reasons he knows.

ABOUT THE AUTHOR

Kirsten Hampton has published articles, stories and poems in literary and academic journals. For her poetry she was a 2017 finalist for the Cider Press Review Book Award judged by Lauren K. Alleyne and a 2018 finalist for the Jean Feldman Poetry Prize. A selection of her poems was also nominated for the Best of the Net. She has received poetry fellowships and residencies from *The Gettysburg Review,* Mid Atlantic Arts Foundation and Virginia Center for the Creative Arts.

The daughter of a composer and painter, and a graduate of Cornell University, Hampton began her career working in British Parliament, U.S. Congress and performing arts institutions. She served for over 10 years in higher education as a Vice President and Associate Dean and later became Chief Operating Officer for a Washington, D.C., think tank. She now partners with her husband in a management and media consulting company, and in making documentary films.

www.kirstenhampton.com